FENG SHUI MADE SIMPLE

Beginning Steps to Harmony

MILLICENT KLINGER-CAMPBELL

To the harmonious energies that bind us, both seen and felt but often unspoken, this journey is a tribute to you.

To my family, whose unwavering support has been my foundation and my peace, you are the joyous laughter that fills every corner of my heart. This work mirrors the comfort of your embrace and the steadfastness of your love.

To my dear friends, who have weathered life's storms by my side, you are the balanced forces that have grounded me when the winds of change threaten my resolve. This handbook is imbued with the strength and resilience you've inspired.

To you, my cherished reader, embarking on this transformative path, may you find solace in these pages. May they be your companion in quiet moments, guiding you through chaos and light, leading you to spaces of serenity and love.

And to the quiet warrior within us all, fighting battles between clutter and clarity, may this book be your shield, strategy, and victory song. With all the love and light within me, I dedicate this handbook to you.

CONTENTS

Introduction

An Author's Tale

By opening this little book, you have embarked on a simple journey to a space that supports your well-being, sparks creativity, and keeps things flowing smoothly.

Welcome to my world of feng shui—where every energy shift is a step toward joy. This book is an invitation to improve your life in many ways. Would you like to move forward with me? I've put this guide together just for you! No special training or skills are required—everything is explained clearly and straightforwardly.

Like a secret waiting to be unveiled, feng shui wasn't just a career twist but a personal awakening for me. A real estate broker in the hustle and bustle of the city, I found serenity in this ancient art. Who knew that organizing homes for sale would evolve into a passion for balancing energies and transforming lives? Forget the jargon that makes you dizzy; we're talking honest advice for real people. I've seen feng shui spark romance, soothe toddlers, and even help sell homes faster than you can say "energy flow."

With an eye for potential and a heart attuned to the subtle rhythms of space, I ventured beyond the realm of curb appeal and square footage. My exploration wasn't through the aisles of scholarly certifications but across the living, breathing tapestry of actual homes and real lives. Each cluttered corner, misplaced table, and joyless space narrated a story, and I listened—absorbing lessons no textbook could teach.

But why keep all the feng shui secrets to myself? Why not share the laughter that bubbles up when you finally let go of that expensive but ghastly vase you never liked? Or the sigh of relief when you create a tranquil nook

just for you? Feng shui is not merely a practice but an experience—sometimes profound, often amusing, but always deeply personal.

This handbook was born from the trenches of cluttered lofts, houses, condos, and bungalows—a companion for the curious and a playbook for the enthusiasts.

Have you ever walked into a room and felt calm, energized, and at ease? That is the magic of feng shui—and the good news is, you don't need to be an expert to create that feeling in your own space! Whether you are totally new to feng shui or looking for a simple way to bring balance to your home, this book is for you. In these pages you'll find easy, beginner-friendly steps to help you organize your space while tapping into the powerful energy of feng shui. No overwhelming rituals, just simple, actionable tips that can make a huge difference in how you feel about your home and your life.

I'm a seeker of harmony, a curator of good vibes, and now your guide on this feng shui journey. The book is not about perfection—it's about making small changes that bring great results! I'll show you how to declutter, arrange furniture, and add little touches that shift the energy around you. Think of it as fun. Together, let's chuckle at the surprises, wade through the mess, and maybe find that spot in our homes where our souls can dance freely.

In these pages you won't just find rules; you'll discover parts of yourself tucked between the lines—your ambitions, fears, and love. Ultimately, feng shui is about coming home to yourself as much as it is about styling a space.

1 WHAT IS FENG SHUI

Secrets to a balanced environment

"Craft an environment that exudes positivity"

What exactly is this mysterious concept called feng shui? It's a question many have pondered, yet few truly understand. You may have heard the term tossed about in conversation or mentioned in articles, but the essence of feng shui remains ambiguous. Let's demystify this ancient art and uncover its secrets.

At its core, feng shui is about achieving balance between yourself and your surroundings. Picture it as a bridge connecting you to your environment, a practice that dates back over three thousand years in the annals of Chinese wisdom. Recently, it has found its place in what we in the West might call the New Age.

Feng shui isn't a religion. It doesn't involve worshiping deities or following dogmas. Instead, it delves into unseen energy, a force known as Chi, the essence of life itself. Think of it as letting this life energy flow freely around you, cultivating a canvas for prosperous living. Feng shui is not a magical cure-all; it's about channeling the unseen energy surrounding us. When harnessed correctly, Chi, the energy of life, promotes well-being and prosperity.

Imagine walking into your home or office and instantly feeling a sense of harmony and joy. That's the power of feng shui. It's the art of crafting an environment that exudes positivity. While it doesn't ascribe to a particular decorating style, it seamlessly integrates with your interior design. Think of it as an invisible hand guiding your choices.

Feng shui means wind and water, reflecting the ancient Chinese pursuit of harmony with the natural world. Chi and feng shui are working at the same time.

Feng shui has evolved and expanded, captivating minds beyond its cultural origin and finding widespread acceptance.

So how does it work? Feng shui operates on the principle that where and how you place objects can influence the energy within a space. We consider what those objects symbolize and the energy they carry. For instance, a strategically placed mirror can redirect energy, a flowing fountain can promote abundance, and symbols of prosperity can invite financial well-being. Symbolic representations help achieve optimal energy flow.

I believe in merging feng shui practices with decluttering and organization. Feng shui isn't a matter of plopping objects around haphazardly; it's about intention. One of the most potent ways to create space for positive energy is by clearing out the clutter. We'll dive deeper into that later.

But here's the truth: while some folks have an innate knack for creating harmonious spaces, most don't quite grasp the art of aligning energy intuitively. That's why feng shui exists—to give us a roadmap to balance our environments and, in turn, our lives. Through simple principles, it enables us to harness the unseen, unique energy surrounding us, a force waiting to be tapped into.

You will discover that feng shui is not a mere tool for improvement but a continuous practice of growth and understanding. It is a testament to living intentionally, so that each adjustment in your home echoes in aspects of your personal and professional life. This creates a symphony of positive energy and profound peace. The journey into feng shui is best walked upon now, enriching your life from this moment forward.

By immersing yourself in feng shui today, you empower yourself to actively influence the here and now, fostering an environment that resonates with comfort, happiness, and health. Of course, this is not medical advice. You must take the advice of your medical professionals, and feng shui will be there to support you. It is a way of taking charge of your living experience and enhancing it to a level where every day feels purposeful. This practice is not just preparation for the future; it's about enriching your present.

So welcome to the world of feng shui, where balance and energy flow meet, and the magic of harmony awaits those seeking it.

Remember, luck in feng shui isn't merely chance; it's a way of aligning yourself with the energies around you, something this book will help you master. Each section of the home, as diagrammed on the Bagua map in chapter 6, can influence that area of your life. For example, I placed a trinket from a loved one in my "helpful people and travel" section. Soon after this I received an invitation to visit friends in London, and another invitation to visit friends in Charleston.

Skeptics say any changes are coincidental; yet, as you witness the transformative power of feng shui principles, such doubts will melt away. These people haven't grasped how feng shui works. You can shift your relationships and attitudes. Everything in the universe turns and assists us when we take the right action.

2 | WHAT IS CHI

Invisible energy that shapes our world

"Carve pathways for Chi to glide freely"

Feel the flow of Chi, the power that connects all of us with the universe!

The concept of Chi is rooted in ancient Chinese wisdom. Imagine a world where this vibrant energy dances through every corner of your life—your cozy abode, bustling office, even that nostalgic attic crammed with memories!

Chi, the heartbeat of existence, pulses with the essence of yin and yang—yin, the gentle touch of femininity, and yang, the bold essence of masculinity. These are the dynamic energies that make it all come alive. A splendid dance between yin and yang is the secret to true harmony. Both need to be equally balanced to bring about their full potential.

This chapter will delve deeper into understanding the nature of Chi, learning to perceive its currents, and mastering the subtle art of navigating its flow. Imagine a stream meandering through a landscape. Nature thrives where the water moves freely; however, where the flow becomes blocked or stagnant, the vitality seeps away, leaving an aura of depletion. Chi operates on a similar principle, imbuing spaces with either positive or negative energy or, when obstructed, creating an atmosphere of negativity. This negativity impacts our well-being, mental clarity, and life quality. Now uncover the secrets to a vibrant life energized by the harmonious rhythm of Chi: one space, breath, and energy shift at a time.

Pause. Inhale tranquility. Exhale distractions. Tune in to the soft stirrings of Chi, a symphony best heard in serenity.

In your realm, carve pathways for Chi to glide freely. Embrace open spaces, inviting this enchanting energy to whirl and twirl, enveloping your surroundings.

By embracing the flow of Chi, you grow with a dynamic universe. Every deliberate action echoes with intention, and every moment promises renewal. Relationships may flourish, inspiration may strike like lightning, and the areas of life once stuck may flow freely once more. You don't need to be a feng shui virtuoso to answer the call. The flow of Chi does not demand monumental shifts for improvement. Understanding Chi is recognizing the profound impact of even the most minute changes.

Not all of us can sense Chi's gentle whispers. Feng shui is an opportunity to learn, grow, and appreciate the dance of energy. That's where the magic comes in.

Chi flows throughout our homes, office spaces, automobiles, and any space belonging to us.

Are you seeking positivity? Then align your treasures with a purpose. Bid farewell to any objects and clutter that dampen the spirit. Even the mundane corner can transform into a haven of vitality with a flick of redesign. You are the curator of your space and consequently the energy that permeates it.

You see, when we follow feng shui we are not just concerned with moving things around. We are orchestrating a vibrant rhythm, a melody of well-being. Small shifts, significant impacts—the power lies in your hands.

Begin by parting with the unnecessary, the excess baggage weighing down your energy. Let go and let Chi breeze through. Farewell to unneeded, unused furniture that cramps the style—sometimes the pieces just don't click.

Chi combined with feng shui is your ally, your guide to a life brimming with radiance. Feel it, embrace it, and let it paint your world in hues of possibility.

3 | WHAT IS CLUTTER
The silent energy drain

"Sentimentality should not imprison you"

Clutter, in essence, is the accumulation of anything that no longer serves a purpose or brings value to your life. It's the excess baggage weighing down your space and your mind. But fear not! Decluttering is the art of liberation, of reclaiming your space and sanity. It is any unfinished project or items you've been hanging onto, not knowing what to do with them. It may even include things that hold emotions yet to be resolved.

The key to unlocking positive energy in your life is decluttering and incorporating feng shui elements. Sometimes both go hand in hand.

Living in a clutter-free environment is bliss! Clutter causes a lack of clarity and impairs self-esteem. It is time to move on to positive living and remove feelings of shame and confusion, allowing clarity to flow freely.

Start by assessing each item in your surroundings. Does it serve a practical function? Does it bring you joy or enhance your environment? If not, it's time to bid the item farewell.

Begin with the apparent offenders—the knickknacks gathering dust, the piles of papers suffocating your desk, the clothes spilling out of your closet. These are the low-hanging fruits of clutter, the easy victories that will fuel your decluttering momentum.

Next, delve deeper. Explore the hidden corners, the forgotten drawers, the shelves obscured by shadows. Here lies the true challenge of decluttering—the emotional attachments, the "what ifs," the "someday maybes." But remember, sentimentality should not imprison you. Keep what truly matters, what truly enriches your life.

As you declutter, envision the space you desire—a sanctuary of serenity, a haven of harmony. Let go of the excess and make room for clarity, creativity, and calm. With each item you release, feel the weight lifting from your shoulders, the energy shifting in your space.

When you've cleared the clutter, bask in the newfound freedom. Revel in the spaciousness, simplicity, and sheer delight of a clutter-free existence. In decluttering your space, you declutter your mind, opening yourself to infinite possibilities and untold joys.

4 | WHY DECLUTTER
Breaking free from disorder

"Create a space that reflects your inner self"

Embarking on the journey to declutter your life doesn't have to be daunting. Remember, the path to a serene and balanced environment is built by taking one small step at a time. The aim is to complete one segment fully before moving on, ensuring thoroughness and a sense of accomplishment. Instead of overwhelming yourself with the entirety of the task, choose to focus on one element of your choice. That might be a drawer or a closet. This method not only makes the process manageable but also provides you with little waves of accomplishment, fueling your motivation to proceed.

As you initiate this process, understand that decluttering is not a one-and-done affair. It's akin to peeling the layers of an onion. You'll likely need to go over the same area several times to refine your space genuinely. The goal is simple: unclog your environment. By clearing tables and surfaces, you immediately witness the creation of physical space and, more important, mental space. Parting with furniture that is no longer functional or aesthetically pleasing can be incredibly liberating.

You'll encounter belongings that tug at your heartstrings, making them hard to part with. Here's a gentle strategy: pack these items in boxes, label them with a date, and store them out of immediate sight. Setting a personal deadline for making a decision helps you reassess the importance of these items. If they remain untouched beyond the date, perhaps it's time to let go of them.

Recognizing that clutter often comprises things that no longer serve a purpose in our lives is crucial. Letting go doesn't mean losing; it's about making room for growth and new opportunities. The fear of making a mistake in what you choose to discard can be paralyzing, but it's essential to trust the process. Removing something signifies a readiness to move on, a necessary step in personal development.

The decluttering expedition is uniquely yours, and it's liberating. You're under no obligation to retain items that don't have pleasant connotations, including those gifts that never quite found a place in your heart. Give yourself the freedom to create a space that reflects your inner self. Furthermore, streamlining doesn't mean stripping away personality. Collections and cherished items can still find their home on your surfaces, but consider unifying them through presentation. Grouping them on trays or in attractive containers can transform what was once visual noise into a harmonious display. Be creative—unexpected items like unique dishes or ornamental bowls can become the perfect vessels for these collections.

Simple changes made with awareness of feng shui can activate powerful benefits. If your environment is not too cluttered when you begin, it works well to do the decluttering and placements simultaneously. Keep the items you love around your home because your home affects your life. In contrast, items that make you sad or that carry reminders of difficult memories can drain your energy if not removed. Free areas of negative energy and add positive energy. Keeping the home balanced requires minimal effort unless it is cluttered and rundown. In this event, decluttering is to be done first and placements next.

You will see benefits as you do the work little by little. Schedule bits of time for this work, and do not try to get everything done in a rush. An essential reminder is not to remove another person's items unless that person specifically asks you to. It is up to the owner to decipher the meaning of each item and consider taking one of the actions mentioned in this chapter.

Remember, every item in your sanctuary should have purpose and intention. By methodically sifting through your environment, you're not just organizing; you're taking a profound journey toward creating a space that nourishes your soul. So take that step—one little victory at a time.

5 | WHERE TO BEGIN

Entryway essentials

"Set the stage for the beautiful chapters ahead"

Dive into the transformative process of revitalizing your home where it all begins—the main entrance. This crucial area bridges your world and the vast expanse beyond, crafting first impressions and setting energetic tones.

Transformation is a journey, not a sprint. Whether you're sprucing up your main entrance or tidying a corner of a room, each effort is a leap toward a harmonious living space, echoing with clarity and inspiration. By embracing this approach, even a modest change can ripple into significant life-enhancing results.

You can transform your home into a beacon of positivity, starting at the main entrance, the heart of your abode. Picture this: every time the door swings open, it's not just you entering the house but also a world of possibilities.

Your main entrance is more than a doorway—it's a prologue to the story of your life, setting the stage for all the beautiful chapters that lie ahead. A clear, welcoming entrance suggests a readiness to embrace the comfort of home and the adventures that await outside it. Imagine what it would be like if every return to your sanctuary wasn't just routine but a little celebration of its own.

Avoid the temptation to let clutter accumulate here. A congested entrance hampers physical movement and stifles your life's momentum and potential growth. An unobstructed doorway, on the other hand, invites an uninterrupted flow of positivity and opportunities.

Now let's add some fun to functionality. How about we make a little game of maintaining a clutter-free space?

Consider each unnecessary item you remove as sweeping away doubt or worry. Picture your entryway as a canvas, and you're the artist. The less clutter there is, the more room you have to paint a vibrant picture filled with joyful opportunities.

And remember, while we're focusing on making this space inviting and lively, it's also a metaphor for your life's path. Your decision about what to keep and what to let go of is choosing what influences you want to allow or release in your life. With every item you discard, you make room for fresh experiences. With every speck of dust you wipe away, you clear the cobwebs off your dreams.

If the thought of a total entrance makeover feels overwhelming, fear not! Small steps are as triumphant as giant leaps. Maybe you choose a new welcome mat today or replace a bulb tomorrow. Each action is a positive affirmation: "I'm ready for happiness and success."

Shed light on your aspirations, literally and metaphorically, by ensuring your entrance is well lit. A gleaming space beckons brightness and clarity into your life, making every homecoming joyful.

Let there be light, and let it be bright! It's incredible how much a well-lit space can boost our spirits. If you're feeling adventurous, why not experiment with different hues of light or playful lighting fixtures? It's all about creating an environment that reflects and magnifies your inner light out into the world.

A clear, welcoming entrance suggests a readiness to embrace the comfort of home and the adventures that await outside its confines. Your home's entrance is the first chapter of your daily adventure story, and together we will make it a page-turner!

6 THE BAGUA MAP

A map to your best life

We're about to unfold the mysteries and joys hidden in the Bagua map, a trove of wisdom that originated in China about three thousand years ago. This is our magical grid blueprint. The Bagua map determines which parts of a home or room correlate with different life circumstances. The center of the home represents the Earth element and should be given special attention to ground the house's energy. Using earthy tones or plants can strengthen this.

The Bagua map is like a treasure map, guiding you to energize each space uniquely. In the heart of your home, the Earth element lays down its roots, setting the stage for the rest of the house. This area is in the northeast sector of any space. Keeping the Earth sector well maintained, and placing items that symbolize wealth there, can help invite prosperity into your life. Make this part of your space a magnet for wealth with lush plants or shiny treasures. Just make sure they're the epitome of health and success!

On the next page you will see a square divided into nine sections, each a domain resonating with specific life energies. But it's not just about spaces; it's about you! Each section mirrors a part of your life, ready to be

THE BAGUA MAP

energized and harmonized. And the key to unlocking
these mysteries lies right in the pages of this handbook.

Imagine stepping into a realm where every corner
of your space is a seed waiting to sprout infinite
possibilities. Ready to dive in? Here we go!

1. **Wealth & Prosperity:** Ever wished for a money
    tree? This zone represents abundance and
    success. Jazz up this area with lush plants or shiny
    crystals and watch the magic of prosperity grow!
    Wherever your kitchen is located, the stove can
    cook up wealth. Ignite every burner to represent
    different income sources. This symbolizes starting
    different revenue streams or bringing in more
    financial energy.

2. **Fame & Reputation:** Ready for your red-carpet
    moment? Ignite this area with fiery elements—
    think reds and bright lights—and feel your
    confidence soar. The energy in this zone affects
    how you're perceived in the world. Shine bright
    like a diamond!

3. **Love & Marriage:** Seeking love or looking to
    rekindle the spark in your relationships? Cozy
    up this corner with pairs of objects and soothing
    artwork. It's essential to have paired items
    (symbolizing any union) in the relationship area of
    your home, which is the farthest right corner from
    the entrance, opposite the wealth corner. Single
    items look lonely. Two candles, side by side, could
    spark the flame of romance. Are you dreaming of
    wedding bells? A photo of a wedding ring might
    just coax destiny your way.

4. **Health & Family:** Nothing tops health and family!
    Wood elements and healthy green plants in this
    section of your home strengthen familial bonds

and keep the energy of well-being flowing. Here's to heart-to-heart chats and laughter that heals!

5. **Center/Earth (Middle):** The heart of everything! This area affects overall life balance. Keep it clean, decluttered, and open to let the good vibes navigate freely. It's the calm amidst life's hustle and bustle.

6. **Creativity & Children:** Unleash your inner Picasso! This zone is all about creative juices and youthful joy. Spruce it up with your artwork or fun do-it-yourself projects—anything that makes your heart sing a playful tune.

7. **Knowledge & Self-cultivation:** Books, tranquility, and maybe a touch of blue or earthy tones can make this corner your sanctuary for growth and self-reflection. Absorb, learn, and expand your horizons.

8. **Career & Life Path:** Where am I going? What are my goals? Infuse this area with inspirational symbols or water elements to navigate life's journey. Keep the energy fluid and inviting for opportunities. In my home, my career and life path are located at the front door. I have placed a water element and a beautiful work of art in the entryway.

9. **Helpful People & Travel:** Need a helping hand or yearning for new adventures? Metallic objects or images of places you want to visit can beckon supportive energies and travel opportunities. Embrace the spirit of exploration!

7 | THE POWER OF COLORS

Palette potency

"Orchestrate your space to resonate with life's melody"

Each section of the Bagua map represents a different life aspect such as home life or career, and by aligning the colors of the map with color areas in your home you can enhance your home's Chi (energy flow). For instance, the Southeast sector relates to wealth and abundance, often harmonized by wood elements and shades of green and purple.

Whether you're keen on inviting love, boosting your wealth, cultivating health, or any other aspect of life, understanding the Bagua areas in your home and incorporating the appropriate colors can create a balanced, harmonious environment. You are orchestrating your surroundings to resonate with your life's melody.

It's fascinating how colors not only add aesthetic value but also have the power to influence our emotions and energy levels. They're like silent pep-talkers, each with its unique personality, sparking a range of emotional responses. Let's dive into this colorful world and see how they can transform our daily experiences, shall we?

Ever felt furious in a crimson room or oddly calm in baby blue? That's no coincidence! Colors are like emotional wizards, casting spells on our feelings.

Blue is your Zen master, bringing in waves of tranquility. Imagine walking into a room bathed in a soothing shade of blue, reminding you of the calm ocean. This color doesn't just please the eye; it's like a gentle pat on the shoulder that eases anxiety and whispers, "Relax, you're safe here." It's no wonder many people choose blue for bedrooms or meditation spaces. It's like having a slice of the serene sky in your corner, promoting tranquility and restful sleep.

Red is the extrovert of the spectrum, radiating energy and passion. It's the color of fire and love, stirring excitement. Have you ever wondered why many dining spaces or restaurants incorporate red elements? Red is a spicy dish that whets the appetite and prompts conversation. A splash of red is perfect for a dull day, but if you coat an entire room, it's a recipe for daily household drama. On the exterior, however, a red front door is said to bring good fortune.

Are you feeling adventurous and warm? Let orange, the social catalyst, take the stage. This fun-loving color boosts feelings of enthusiasm and can turn any living room into a lively lounge for happy gatherings. Orange is the social butterfly that gets everyone talking and laughing together. It's like perpetual autumn in your space, without the falling leaves!

Yellow is your loyal companion if you aim for a cheerful, sunny vibe that uplifts your spirit. This color mimics sunshine, promoting happiness, optimism, and mental clarity. Kitchens, living areas, or study spaces would love some yellow cheer. It's like walking into a room filled with positive affirmations.

For those who seek a touch of luxury and creativity, purple makes a grand entrance. Often associated with royalty, this color can turn any space into an elegant, imaginative haven. Purple encourages deep thinking and sensitivity. It is a perfect accent for areas where you're artistic and reflective.

In contrast, white is the minimalist's best friend. It speaks of purity, simplicity, and peace. It's like a blank canvas, offering mental clarity and an open invitation to add splashes of any color that reflects your personality. White is particularly appealing for home offices or spaces where you must think, focus, and innovate.

And who can forget charming pink? This color seems to bestow a tender, loving hug. It's all about affection, kindness, and comfort. Want love to bloom? Pink is your Cupid, making bedrooms feel like romantic oases. This color promotes feelings of romance and tranquility. It's like surrounding yourself with love notes!

Colors are silent storytellers, transforming our living spaces into sanctuaries that echo our emotions, aspirations, and inner peace. What's your story, and which color will help you tell it?

Your space is not just a physical area but a vibrant echo of your inner world. And with the Bagua map from this handbook, you're an orchestra conductor, creating a symphony of energies in perfect harmony. So, roll up your sleeves, let your imagination run wild, and start crafting the life you wish to live, one section at a time!

8 | THE FIVE ELEMENTS
Elemental synergy

"Arrange the elements to align with your aspirations"

The Five Elements of feng shui invoke the energies that influence our emotions, behaviors, and perspectives. They extend far beyond decor. By understanding and implementing the Five Elements, you invite into your space a dance of natural forces that harmonize with your inner self, offering a sanctuary that aligns with your life's rhythm and aspirations.

The Five Elements aren't just random objects but influential conductors of energy that can make your home feel like a harmonious concert. The trick is in the balance, like a superhero team bringing out the best in each other. Wood fuels Fire, Fire creates Earth, and Earth forges Metal—an elemental saga in your living room!

Below is a detailed explanation of each feng shui element, paired with specific items that can embody it in your space.

1. **FIRE:** Illuminating and Invigorating

Meaning: The Fire element signifies radiance, passion, and dynamism. It's an energy booster, encouraging solid social connections, enthusiasm, and motivation.

In Feng Shui: Implementing Fire elements can stimulate inspiration, emotional expressiveness, and social openness. These elements fuel ambition and help acknowledge one's power.

Representative Items: Candles, lamps, lighting fixtures, and items in fiery colors (reds, oranges, purples) or triangular shapes. Images of sunlight or vibrant landscapes can also amplify the Fire element.

2. **EARTH:** Stabilizing and Nurturing

Meaning: The Earth element embodies stability, nourishment, and calm grounding, promoting care and solid support within your environment.

In Feng Shui: Earth elements enhance relaxation, healing, and security. They foster clear, practical thinking and the systematic achievement of goals.

Representative Items: Objects made of clay or brick, ceramics, square shapes, and imagery of landscapes. Colors like light yellow and brown tones also invoke the Earth element.

3. **METAL:** Refining and Clarifying

Meaning: Metal reflects clarity, precision, and a crisp lucidity, encouraging sharpness in intellect and streamlined efficiency in activities.

In Feng Shui: Metal creates an atmosphere that promotes better focus, organization, and introspection, cultivating qualities necessary for refinement and improvement.

Representative Items: Metallic objects; sculptures; round shapes; white, gold, or silver decor. Even simple, minimalist pieces can effectively represent Metal energy.

4. **WATER:** Soothing and Connecting

Meaning: Water symbolizes the flow of connectivity, depth, communication, and ease of movement and exchange in various aspects of life.

In Feng Shui: Water elements foster a peaceful environment for deep thinking, clear-mindedness, effective communication, and wise decision-making.

Representative Items: Mirrors, reflective surfaces, fountains, or decor in shades of black or dark blue. Art depicting water scenes can also serve as a representation.

5. **WOOD:** Growing and Vitalizing

Meaning: Wood is the essence of growth, expansion, and the natural progression of life forces. It signifies health, vitality, and a consistent upward energy or change.

In Feng Shui: Wood elements promote personal growth, inspiration, and creative energies. They support health and renewal and leave you feeling rooted yet free to expand.

Representative Items: Wooden furniture or decor, green plants, columnar or rectangular shapes, and green or brown color palettes. Images of lush forests or trees can also bring in Wood energy.

Incorporating these items doesn't mean overhauling your space. You can start with one area and introduce select pieces that resonate with the energies you want to enhance. The key lies in balance, ensuring no single element overwhelms another. This will help maintain harmony that resonates with a room's visible and invisible aspects. Through these incorporations, you create a space and an ecosystem that vibrates with positive, life-affirming energy.

The exterior appearance of your home is as important as the interior. A manicured garden and a lemon tree bursting with zesty fruits invite admiring looks, welcome your guests, and inspire neighbors to keep their own properties beautiful. Lemon trees are considered suitable for attracting cheerful Chi. As people enter your home, they should be greeted with natural indoor plants. Real plants are preferable to fake because they purify the air, promote genuine energy flow, and shower your home with freshness.

Remember, the key to effective feng shui is intentionality. In making physical rearrangements or decor choices, you are setting positive intentions and being transparent about what you want to manifest in your life. Mindfully arranging your space, you align more closely with your life goals and invite positive changes.

9 | POWER POSITIONS AND PLACEMENTS

Small adjustments for major impact

"Dance with the elements and choreograph a vibrant life"

Let's dive into the realm of the power position, a fundamental principle of feng shui. Picture yourself as the king or queen of your castle, facing the main door, ready to greet opportunity as it waltzes in. Your throne—your favorite chair or couch—should never turn its back on the door. That's like turning away good fortune itself! Command your space with the poise of royalty; after all, your kingdom thrives on your strength and control.

The power position advises positioning furniture, especially seating areas, to face the room's entrance. This reduces any feeling of vulnerability and promotes a sense of security.

Understanding the concept of power positions is key to unlocking your energy flow. A power position is about positioning yourself where you feel secure, supported, and in control, having a clear view of your surroundings. These strategic placements help you feel more balanced, confident, and in command of your space and your life. When you are in a power position, you feel empowered, and you are sending a message to the universe that you are ready to take charge of your destiny!

Seating placement is vital in dining, living, or other rooms. When setting up chairs and sofas, you should aim to sit where you can quickly see everyone in the room. This helps you feel more in control of conversations and situations.

In the living room, avoid placing furniture that forces you to have your back to the door. This creates a sense of unease. Instead, position the seating to face the entrance or at least have a clear view so you're always aware of the people who enter and exit.

By understanding power positions and incorporating them into your life, you align yourself with the natural energy flow around you.

There is never a wrong time to begin the journey of transformation. Be explicit about what you want to accomplish, and commit to the pull to initiate new beginnings. As you notice the positive changes in your life, feng shui becomes a process of continuous improvement.

Embarking on this journey is like setting sail on a sea of life-changing energy. You're not just decorating; you're setting powerful intentions. Each adjustment is a dialogue with the universe, a step toward a home that mirrors your dreams and ambitions. So why wait? Dive in, dance with the elements, and let feng shui choreograph a waltz of vibrant life all around you!

10 CONCRETE STEPS TO GUIDE YOU

Here are a few simple tips. They are not in any particular order. Feel free to follow them in any sequence that works for you.

If the house is cluttered, start decluttering before organizing and applying feng shui. This will make space for new energy.

Walk through your home. The area that bothers you the most is a good place to start decluttering.

Start with one area and complete the entire area before beginning another.

If space constraints or the configuration of your home do not allow you to make all the placements diagrammed on the Bagua map, do not worry. Nothing negative will come of it.

Many items in a home can be used in different rooms—bedroom, kitchen, office. Don't be hesitant to move items from their traditional places to other rooms.

Let go of duplicates that you never use.

Don't save items for special occasions; use them daily for your enjoyment.

When cleaning wardrobe closets, remember what you wear says a lot about you. Keep clothing and shoes that are comfortable, stylish, and in excellent shape. Less is more.

Let go of outdated, unloved, unusable, or unflattering apparel and accessories.

It's best to use live, healthy plants, but if there is not enough light, you may use artificial plants indoors. Just make sure they are kept very clean.

Be careful not to use broken items as symbols when making placements. This will bring negative energy.

Do not keep things behind doors. Allow all doors in the home to open completely.

Do not move or discard someone else's possessions without that person's permission. The owner's energy is embedded in them.

It's not a good idea to rent a storage unit or store things in your attic, garage, or basement. Your energy is tied up in all your possessions, and when you must store items, it shows that they no longer serve a purpose in your life.

If you use something, put it right back. If you eat something, put the dish directly in the dishwasher. If you drop something, pick it up.

Keeping your home or office organized is less work than letting mail, paperwork, and projects pile up.

Mail and paperwork create messes if not attended to immediately. Designate a place to put the mail if you plan to handle it later. For example, buy matching baskets for everyone in your home and sort the mail into them. That will help keep counters, desks, and furniture uncluttered and expedite handling of the mail.

Conclusion

May your home nurture your soul on this ongoing journey. With mindfulness and intention, your environment can bring harmony between your inner world and the universe.

Clearing clutter and welcoming positive energy allows new opportunities and joy to flow freely, creating space for physical and emotional transformation.

Creating balance invites grace, emotional well-being, and a sense of peace into your life. Every small change you make shifts the energy around you, helping to support your deepest intentions and spiritual growth.

Trust the process, embrace the energy, and allow balance to unfold.

www.ingramcontent.com/pod-product-compliance
Lightning Source LLC
Chambersburg PA
CBHW061101050726
47592CB00004B/1780